THAT GLIMPSE OF TRUTH FOR WHICH YOU HAD FORGOTTEN TO ASK

Uroboric Apperception and Psychotherapy:
Some Thoughts on the *Mise en Scène* Character
of the True Subject

GREG MOGENSON

A publication of
The International Society for Psychology as the Discipline of Interiority
Monograph Series, vol. 3

Cover design by Michael Mendis

ISBN: 9781794030879

SOURCES AND ABBREVIATIONS

The following abbreviations have been used for frequently cited sources:

CEP: Wolfgang Giegerich, *The Collected English Papers of Wolfgang Giegerich*, 6 vols., New Orleans: Spring Journal Books, 2005-2013. Cited by volume and page number.

CW: Carl Gustav Jung, *Collected Works*, 20 vols. Herbert Read, Michael Fordham, Gerhard Adler and William McGuire, eds., R. F. C. Hull, trans., Princeton: Princeton University Press, 1957-1979. Cited by volume and paragraph number.

CHAPTER TOPICS AND THEMES

I

Facts psychology ψ Its forgetfulness of truth ψ Joseph Conrad's view of art ψ Freud's one neurosis heuristic ψ Jung's "higher psycho-therapy" ψ Listening-based interpretation versus psycho-education

II

Quotes from Jung resonate with Conrad's truth-discerning acuity of art ψ Connecting the dots ψ Leaving Oedipus, the libido, and the unconscious behind ψ Truth, soul, and justice as the aims of a speculative process ψ From Freud and Jung to Giegerich and PDI

III

Psychology's rootedness in the *notion* of soul ψ The psychological difference ψ The soul, being notional, is always whole ψ Holding Proteus until he prophecies ψ Parable of the lost sheep ψ "What thou doest to the least of these brethren of mine you also do to me" ψ The comprehensive and all-fathoming character of the soul ψ Negated exceptions included in its logical life ψ Not a theory of everything ψ The soul's meeting itself in phenomena that are the mediating exponents of all they are not ψ "The stone that is not a stone" ψ Giegerich's wilderness metaphor ψ Actaion and Artemis ψ The situation as a whole writ small ψ Seeing from outside contrasted with seeing from within

IV

Conrad on the artist's task ψ The presented vision of regret, or pity, terror or mirth ψ Evocation of solidarity ψ Jung on the "picture that looms up, covered by a thin veil of facts" ψ Psychology in the usual sense of "what goes on inside people" outstripped ψ Jung's "supra-individual psyche" ψ Psychology's lack of an Archimedean vantagepoint ψ *Psychological* psychology ψ The psychic situation seen from within, under the aspect of Archimedeanlessness

V

Jung on overcoming the consulting room mentality ψ Psychology's meeting itself in other disciplines ψ Positivistic treatments limited to what's "going on under the hood" ψ Archimedeanless immersion in "the third of the two" ψ The analogy to dreams ψ "Meet[ing] ourselves … in a thousand disguises on the path of life" (Jung) ψ Psychology's falling between the academic stools ψ The psychotherapist's need for knowledge of the general human mind ψ Wandering with a human heart through the world ψ The self-othering character of the soul ψ Absolute exposure and the disclosing of truth

VI

Our "appear[ing] wondrously strange to ourselves" ψ Jung's travels in North Africa ψ His dream of wrestling with an Arab prince ψ The sighting of a youth that inspired Conrad's *Lord Jim* ψ Jim apperceived by Marlow as "an individual in the forefront of his kind … affect[ing] mankind's conception of itself" ψ The industrial revolution and the decline of the sense of duty and traditional meaning ψ Conrad's *The Nigger of the Narcissus* ψ The negative mediation of inwardness ψ Hegel's speculative remark ψ From the majesty of wind power to the indignity of shoveling coal ψ From duty to worker's rights ψ Nietzsche and nihilism ψ The closing of an era

VII

Uroboric psychotherapy ψ The Archimedeanlessness of psychology ψ The eyes through which consciousness visits gazes upon itself ψ Jung's "Concerning Rebirth" ψ "One becomes Two" (Nietzsche) ψ Risk and consequence, courage and cowardice ψ The psychological difference, weakly read ψ No way to get from the ego to "the soul" ψ Sticking with the image, the dream, the apperceptive surround ψ "The greater part

6

of the soul … is outside the body" ψ A voice in the wilderness is heard to cry "I"

VIII

S. T. Coleridge ψ "the snake with its Tail in its Mouth" ψ Uroboric psychotherapy ψ Hegel's speculative sentence ψ Conrad on art, Jung on "the higher psychotherapy" ψ The *truth* of psychotherapy ψ *"Animae extra corpus est"*

MAIOR AUTEM ANIMAE [PARS] EXTRA CORPUS EST[1]

[the larger part of the soul, however, is outside the body]

I

WITHOUT A DOUBT when broadly defined to include all the various kinds of itself—from academic and clinical psychology, through psychoanalysis, behaviorism and the rest—psychology knows a tremendous amount about "the facts of life." It knows about reflexes and conditioned responses; about memory, perception, and learning; about sexuality and attachment behaviour; about family dynamics and our development through the life-cycle; about addiction, trauma, and the brain, and a whole lot more besides. But what about "that glimpse of truth for which you had forgotten to ask"? Does it know about that?

The phrase I have just cited comes from a little essay of Joseph Conrad's in which the great novelist discusses what he regards as being the main thrust of artistic endeavour.[2] Art, in this author's view, is the aesthetically realized expression of "a single-minded attempt to render the highest kind of justice to the visible universe, by bringing to light the truth, manifold and one, underlying its every aspect." Elaborating upon this statement, he continues, "It is an attempt to find in its forms, in its colours, in its lights, in its shadows, in the aspects of matter and in the facts of life what of each is fundamental, what is enduring and essential—their own illuminating and convincing quality—the very truth of their existence."[3]

Now surely it is because psychotherapy may also be practiced as an art that I was moved to underline these sentences of Conrad's when first I came upon them. Conceived along similar lines, psychotherapy is also a truth-seeking adventure. It, too, a matter of discerning "in the facts of [a] life what of each is fundamental, … — the very truth of their existence."

But here now, having stated this, I must immediately add, that with this comparison I am only referring to what, with an expression of Jung's, may be called "the higher psychotherapy"[4]—and not to those other kinds of therapeutic pursuit that are so mired in clinical literalism that they cannot see "the forest for the trees," let alone the soul in the matter at hand. That Conrad's statement accords with this is evident in the fact that each of its phrases return us to that higher level or greater dimension of our own endeavor by bringing comparable ideas from our own tradition to mind. His speaking, for example, in the passage I just cited, of "a single-minded attempt," "manifold and one," to "render the highest kind of justice" to whatever its problem or subject matter may be is resonate with similar statements from the depth psychological literature, generally, and from our own literature, in particular. Already in Freud, to start with him, this focus of Conrad's is seconded by that first analyst's view that in each case there is only one neurosis which manifests itself in a myriad of ways. Only consider, if you will, how different the effort to discern this manifold oneness is from the prevailing idea in psychotherapy today that "a piece of work" can be done on this issue or that, without the peas ever needing to touch the carrots, or the chickens ever having to come home to roost. Dispensing what it calls its "evidence-based," but only statistically-valid general knowledge to patients who are already identified with those of its findings that can be picked up from lifestyle magazines and internet searches, psychology has largely set listening and interpretation aside and put psycho-education in their place. Little wonder, then, that Conrad's line about "that glimpse of truth for which you had forgotten to ask" should strike such a chord within us. It is the very thing that's been lost sight of in our information age.[5]

II

A moment ago, I let the passage we began with from Conrad remind me of Freud's teaching that in each case there is only one neurosis, and not a mix of issues abstractly different from one another. Moving on to Jung, I will now cite some texts of his that come as readily to mind. In a lengthy case study in which he discusses the fantasy material of a highly creative American woman,[6] Jung declares that "the *tertium comparationis* for all these symbols is the libido, and the unity of meaning lies in the fact that they are all analogies for the same thing."[7] In another place, Jung makes again much the same point when he states that "the unconscious, being unknown, coincides with itself everywhere."[8] I will not pause to expound upon the ways in which these statements resonate with our phrases from Conrad on the truth-discerning acuity of art, but will simply allow myself to be reminded of another. This, as we shall see, has also to do with the self-referential, or as this might also be called, the connecting-the-dots character of psychological thought and insight. Just as for Jung "the unity of meaning lies in the fact that all [the seemingly diverse symbols in the case he had analyzed] are ... analogies for the same thing," and just as, likewise, "the unconscious, being unknown, corresponds with itself everywhere," so it is also the case that "... in any psychological discussion we are not saying anything *about* the psyche, but ... the *psyche is always speaking about itself.*"[9]

The point to be grasped from this juxtaposing of texts is that those I cited from Jung and alluded to from Freud, no less than the one about art I began with from Conrad, have also to do with a truth-discerning cognitive process. This is not to say, however, that their formulations of this process are free of inhibitions, flawless, and fully fledged. While Freud, for example, provided a great inducement to psychological thinking with his advice about there being in each case only one neurosis, the heuristic power of this idea was needlessly curtailed by his not leaving *what* the neurosis might be about completely open, but rather thinking of it in terms of the Oedipus complex.[10] And a similar criticism may be levelled against Jung for having resorted to positing a subject behind the subjectivity he wanted to explain,[11] "the libido" in the one text and of "the unconscious" in the other.[12] All these referents can be dispensed with, however, Oedipus, *the* libido, and *the* unconscious left behind. For, far from being the already existing *agents* of an empirical process, our own preferable, and I would add, only seemingly less rigorous terms—truth, soul, and justice, too—are the *aims* of an openly speculative one.[13] On each interpretative occasion, whatever the material to be interpreted may be, these come, if they come at all, as the *result* of the kind of thinking process that all the statements I have cited have in common with each other, when those other terms I mentioned are allowed to drop away.

Now with the last of these reflections, the statement we began with from Conrad may be passed like a relay baton from Freud and Jung to Giegerich and PDI.[14] For as we shall see, it is also the view of that contemporary analyst, as it is of the branch of analytical psychology that takes its cue from him, that psychology involves, or more than that, *is constituted by*, the previously mentioned "single-minded attempt," "manifold and one," to " render the highest kind of justice" to whatever the matters it is consulted about may be.

III

The first text I would like to mention in this regard follows from what I said above about leaving (to name only these) "Oedipus," "the libido," and that other fallaciously-posited subject behind subjectivity, "the unconscious," behind in order that a cognitive process may get under way that is open enough to whatever the phenomena quickening it to life may be that *truth* has a chance of being produced, *soul* of being made, *justice* of being done, and the patient of saying "I." In *The Soul's Logical Life*, Giegerich accomplishes this by offering, in place of those too presumption-laden and entity-like conceptions of soul that Freud and Jung, beneath the *niveau* of a truly *psychological* psychology,[15] had resorted to at times, a *notion* of soul that consists of *nothing other than notionality as such*. But let me spell this out. After briefly explaining that "the soul of a theory is the Notion or Concept whose unfolding the theory is," Giegerich offers that "[p]sychological theory is a singular case" in that "[p]sychology is the only discipline in which the life-giving *soul* of the theory happens to be the Notion *of soul* and where what it is the notion *of* is itself nothing other than *Notion*." Continuing, he then boldly declares that "soul is Notion." Now it is important to emphasize that the notion that soul *is* "is not the notion of an empirical 'factor' called 'soul,'" let alone, we might add, of one or the other of those aforementioned empirical factors, the Oedipus complex, the libido, and the unconscious. For as Giegerich further stipulates, "the soul does not exist (out there in 'reality')," in the manner of an entity or thing, but "is only ... *logical*, 'just' a Notion, a thought, a word" that, and this is most crucial, "refers to nothing outside of itself, [but] only to the notion or thought that it means *within* itself or posits in and through itself."[16]

Notice here the difference that is drawn between the empirical and the logical. Like the difference I mentioned earlier between facts and truth, or as I also put this, between psycho-education, on the one hand, and listening-based interpretation, on the other, this difference is a variant of what has come to be called the psychological difference.[17] On the one side of what, when it is opened up, establishes this difference (let's call it, its empirical/factual side) we have the vast array of existing things and experiences that are the stuff of our lives and world. On the other side (let's call it the logical/notional side) we have by contrast (or rather, not by contrast, for that would imply an already existing difference, but by something akin to that episode in *The Odyssey* where Menelaus holds the shape-shifting god, Proteus, until he prophesies![18]) what Conrad called "the singled-minded attempt" to thinkingly discern what is "manifold and one" in the matter or matters at hand. Putting all this another way, let it simply be said that while the world is filled with an enormous variety of independent and interdependent entities and things (and the same can be said for the psychic world of our inner, composed as it is of such contents as memories, feelings, emotional states, complexes, fantasies and the like), "the soul," being notional, is always whole.[19] This is not to say, that it cannot, like a drop of mercury, present itself in a dispersed manner, as internally different from itself, in the form of many smaller drops. Rather, it is to realize (jumping back together again!) that each smaller drop is the whole soul presenting itself to itself in the particularity of one of its moments. And this, I suspect, is pretty much what Jesus was getting at when he told that parable about the shepherd leaving his flock of ninety-nine sheep to find the one lost sheep,[20] or again, when he stated that "what thou doest to the least of these brethren of mine you also do to me."[21] For being of concept-character, soul is always all-fathoming and comprehensive. Equal to itself in all that it reflects itself in or grasps itself as, the thought as which it *is* must include everything in itself, even its negating exceptions, which of course means changing itself up and expanding its grasp in the course of that process we call its logical life. And in connection to this, I am reminded of Giegerich's statement that "What at first appears as a content [or object] of consciousness is in truth the seed of what wants to become a new form of consciousness at large."[22]

But here I should clear up a possible misunderstanding. What I just said about the soul—that it is all-fathoming, comprehensive, and conceptually a whole—is not to imply some sort of theory of everything. The mind of God, we may suppose, would be capable of that, but not psychology or the psychologist. And yet, as before with the statements I quoted from Jesus, something essential about the soul can be learned from such biblical adages as that one about God hearing the sparrow fall.[23] Heir to this proclivity of its religious precursor, what we may now interchangeably refer to as psychology or "the soul" meets itself, ever and again, in those particular phenomena, that, like alchemy's "stone that is not a stone,"[24] are the mediating exponents of all that they are *not*. It is a matter, then, not of a theory of everything, but of a concept of no-thing, or as Giegerich puts it, of concept per se. What Conrad called "that glimpse of truth for which you had forgotten to ask" is sighted in particular matters of interest that, far from being only what they literally or empirically are, are the negative precipitate of their wider cultural context and historical locus. Underscoring this point with another text from our psychological literature, I think of Giegerich's use of the mythological story of Actaion and Artemis and of the metaphor of "wilderness" to discuss the cognition of truth.[25] The wilderness, in Giegerich's view, can be any particular situation, so long as we enter it wholeheartedly and are exposed to it fully.[26] With regards to this, he then makes the important further point that when the wilderness is apperceived as an infinite expanse surrounding us on all sides, we are still only seeing it from outside and not yet glimpsing truth. But when, like Actaion, we are *really* out there, *totally exposed*, it shows itself to us from within; in the myth he is discussing, as Artemis,[27] in our lives, perhaps, as some niggling doubt or unlikely dream figure that we are loath to waste a thought on, except that we know it is our situation as a whole writ small, the insight that we need in its Ugly Duckling, Cinderella, or lapis *in via ejectus/exilis* form.[28]

IV

Returning to our novelist, let us glean a little more for ourselves from his account of the artist's way of finding into truth. Elaborating upon this topic in the same essay, Conrad offers that it is the task of the artist "To snatch in a moment of courage, from the remorseless rush of time, a passing phase of life" and to present this so vividly that it can be heard, felt, and above all, seen. Working to this end, "the task," he continues, "is to hold up unquestioningly, without choice or fear, the rescued fragment before all eyes in the light of a sincere mood. It is to show its vibration, its colour, its form; and through ... [these] reveal the substance of its truth—disclose its inspiring secret: the stress and passion within the core of each convincing moment." Following upon these words, the novelist then offers that it is by means of a "single-minded attempt of [this] kind ... [that] one may perchance attain to such clearness of sincerity that at last the presented vision of regret or pity, of terror or mirth, shall awaken in the hearts of the beholders that feeling of unavoidable solidarity; of the solidarity in mysterious origin, in toil, in joy, in hope, in uncertain fate, which binds men to each other and all mankind to the visible world."[29]

What Conrad here says about art calls to mind similar statements from Jung about the way soul gives rise to itself. First among these is a line from *The Visions Seminars*: "... behind the impressions of the daily life—behind the scenes—another picture looms up, covered by a thin veil of facts."[30] Frequently cited in our literature on account of its being indicative of the psychological difference, this line has in its immediate context to do with the interpretation of dreams. Like the art-forms discussed by Conrad, dreams have an all-encompassing pictorial quality. Drawn at least in part from the impressions of daily life, they, too, express the soul in terms of a "presented vision," or as Jung sometimes calls it, a *mise en scène*, that completely outstrips psychology in the usual sense of what goes on inside people.[31] But here, with this last point, I am getting ahead of myself. At this juncture, it is enough to appreciate the dovetailing of Conrad's point about art being a "presented vision" evocative of an "unavoidable solidarity ... which binds men to each other and all mankind to the visible world" and Jung's about the picture to the power of two that looms up from a dream that is being reflected upon.[32] And here, apropos of this, I am immediately reminded of a statement of Jung's that cinches this comparison. In his essay, "The Structure of the Psyche," Jung states that "If this supra-individual psyche exists, everything that is translated into its picture-language would be depersonalized, and if this became conscious would appear to us *sub specie aeternitatis*. Not as my sorrow, but as the sorrow of the world; not as personal isolating pain, but a pain without bitterness that unites all humanity. The healing effect of this needs no proof."[33]

Many more passages could be cited on the heels of this one that are just as indicative of Jung's unique psychological vision. In the next section, I will cite a few of these, but first I want to unpack the one just quoted.

Jung speaks of a "supra-individual psyche" which effects (and I would add, is produced by) a negating "translat[ion]" wherein all manner of themes and subject matters are portrayed in a de-personalized, i.e., universalizing manner. Just as in a line of his poetry W. B. Yeats can state that, "A girl arose that had red mournful lips/And seemed the greatness of the world in tears,"[34] so Jung refers to a picture-language that depicts "Not ... my sorrow, but ... the sorrow of the world; not ... personal isolating pain, but a pain without bitterness that unites all humanity." The point to be grasped is that here again, as before with his previously mentioned reference to the other picture that looms up, the psychological difference is drawn, this time very explicitly, as the difference between the individual with his or her personal psychology, on the one hand, and what Jung will go on to call the archetypal images of the objective psyche, on the other.

But what about the part of Jung's statement asserting that the depersonalized images of the supra-individual psyche appear to us under the aspect of eternity, or as he puts it, "*sub specie aeternitatis*"? This phrase, I would urge, need not be taken literally, as a highfalutin metaphysical statement, but rather, descriptively, metaphorically, poetically, within the context and economy of Jung's great insight into psychology's lack of an objective Archimedean vantagepoint outside its own phenomenology. Now what this involves can be readily explained by contrasting psychology in the acute sense to which Jung advanced with all those other sciences that operate with a clear difference between the observing subject, on the one hand, and an externally-existing object, on the other. Completely different from these, a truly *psychological* psychology begins with, and develops as the fathoming of, the insight that everything that is said about the psyche is at the same time an expression of the psyche. This, of course, applies to the passages I have been quoting from Jung, as it will again to the others from him I'll be turning to in a moment. These, as we shall see, are also redolent of this lack of an Archimedean point. So much so, in fact, that an inwardness that is not the simple opposite of the outer and external—which is also to say, a subjectivity that is not the simple opposite of the objective—is opened up and bodied forth. And it follows from this that "the other picture that looms up" (be it in analysis when we are listening to our patients or interpreting dreams, or when in the arts we are creating or appreciating works of art) is appearing to us *under the aspect of Archimedeanlessness!* Which means that far from being viewed as a thing-like entity from some objective standpoint outside the psychic process, the depersonalized, universalized, supra-individual image is the exquisitely specific expression of the entirety of the psychic situation as seen from within. As such it is not a thing among other things, but more poetically, more angelically than that, having been raised to the power of all that it is not, the inwardness or truth, "manifold and one," of the psychic situation as a whole, in Giegerich's terms, the Artemis that shows herself when, exposed to what is, we are really in the wild.

V

I said that Jung's statement about the supra-individual psyche reminded me of others. Turning to these now, let us appreciate as we do so their manner of bringing to life the ideas we have been discussing thus far.

I begin arbitrarily with a few lines of Jung's that follow upon his again making the point that "the human psyche ... [is] not only the object but also the subject"[35] of the interest taken in it. After issuing this reminder with respect to what I am calling the Archimedean-lessness of psychology, he then robustly declares that "analytical psychology has burst the bonds which till then had bound it to the consulting-room of the doctor."[36] This bursting of the bonds, which Jung also refers to as "it[s] go[ing] beyond itself,"[37] has to do with psychology's surpassing itself as a mere clinical enterprise, redolent of the medical model, and finding more of itself in whatever "the other" that it meets itself *in* or engages itself *as* may be. For the patient this means an approach to the treatment that is not limited to what is "going on under the hood," so to speak, in the world-less machinations of his clinically-isolated inner,[38] but that transcending itself as this takes into its purview what may variously be called his *mise en scène*, life-world, or apperceptive surround.[39] The readiest analogy to this, of course, is the mutually-constituting relation between the figure of the dream-I and the dream in which it appears.[40] Just as the figure resembling the dreamer is Archimedeanlessly-immersed in the scenes of the dream, so in psychotherapy there are moments when the patient and therapist are Archimedeanlessly-immersed in a "third of the two"[41] that presents itself via the aforementioned "picture that

19

looms up," on the one hand, and the amplifications appropriate to this, on the other.[42] But dreams, as I said, are just an analogy here, merely a vivid way of illustrating Jung's bonds-bursting, consulting-room transcending insight that it is not the psyche that is in us, but rather, we that are in the psyche.[43] For even when dreams are not presented, there is a way of conducting psychotherapy as if they had been[44]—which is also to say, as if "the psyche," "the unconscious," and the "inner world" were not in the patient, but around him, in the form of the events that befall him, the persons he encounters, the situations he must live, as well as the metaphors and stories in terms of which the confines of the consulting room are left behind. And here, as I reflect upon this point, I am prompted to recall Jung's great statement about our "mee[ting] ourselves ... in a thousand disguises on the path of life."[45]

What I just said about the patient holds for psychology as well. Leaving the consulting room mentality behind, if not the actual consulting room, it, too, must meet itself in the wider world, in the guise, for example, of the other sciences. That this is the case follows from Jung's recognition that psychology has no "delimited field,"[46] but "fall[s] between ... the academic stools" inasmuch as the human psyche "forms at least half the ground necessary for the existence of them all."[47]   But is this appreciated? Jung laments that "the doctors interested in psychotherapy have practically no knowledge of the general human mind as it expresses itself in history, archaeology, philology, philosophy and theology, etc., ..."[48] Possession of such knowledge by psychotherapists, however, as dilettantish as it may seem to specialists of those other fields (Jung once described himself as "the most accursed dilettante that has ever lived"[49]), is indispensable, for without its amplifying contribution the fact that, as Jung puts it, "only the smallest part of the psyche ... presents itself in the medical consulting room"[50] cannot be grasped and compensated for. Of course, in working this way, we analysts will "disturb and anger the theologian no less than the philosopher, the physician no less than the educator; … [and] grope about in the fields of the biologist and of the historian." But as Jung explains, "this extravagant behaviour is due not to arrogance [on the part of psychology and the psychologist] but to the circumstance that man's psyche is a unique combination of factors which are at the same time the special subjects of far-reaching lines of research. For it is out of himself and out of his peculiar constitution that man has produced his sciences. They are *symptoms* of his psyche."[51]

Now what we just heard from Jung about the speculative proclivity of psychology to find more of itself in the other sciences extends to all spheres of human endeavor. Using its Archimedean-lessness as a passport or travel visa, it is by venturing into these, whatever they may be, that it finds into its fullness as "a psychology 'with soul.'"[52] And here I am reminded of what is perhaps Jung's most wilderness-entering statement on this topic. Writing in a manner that, on the one hand, squares nicely with what we heard from of Conrad about the discerning of truth in literary art, and, on the other, with those dreams we sometimes have that place us in the most unexpected and at times even exotic settings, Jung declares that

> Anyone who wants to know the human psyche will learn next to nothing from experimental psychology. He would be better advised to put away his scholar's gown, bid farewell to his study, and wander with human heart through the world. There, in the horrors of prisons, lunatic asylums and hospitals, in drab suburban pubs, in brothels and gambling-hells, in the salons of the elegant, the Stock Exchanges, Socialist meetings, churches, revivalist gatherings and ecstatic sects, through love and hate, through the experience of passion in every form in his own body, he would reap richer stores of knowledge than text-books a foot thick could give him, and he will know how to doctor the sick with real knowledge of the human soul.[53]

Jung's point is well-taken. It is clearly the case that a wide experience of life is a boon to the psychotherapist. But there is more to this passage than that. The spirit of adventure evoked in it by Jung, together with the settings and life-situations he mentions, conduct to the important further insight that *the soul is self-othering, self-encountering.* And here it may be added, that leaving behind the tendency of his discipline to reduce itself in the manner of a stay-at-home or a stick-in-the mud to its self-identity as a clinical practice, the adventurous psychologist described in this passage is as much a poet or a novelist as he is a doctor and psychotherapist. For, indeed, there is a strong affinity between the knowledge of the soul that Conrad and his readers have gleaned from his real and imaginary adventures at sea and the knowledge that psychologists and their patients glean from their real and dream-mediated forays into settings such as those Jung describes. In both cases such insight is achieved only as the self-negating, self-sublating result of consciousness having exposed itself wholeheartedly to the settings or situations it apperceives itself to be in.[54] Only when we have been "really out there," fully the exponents of the consciousness we exist both as and in, can the situation be glimpsed from within, its truth disclosed.

VI

But how, more precisely, does such insight first present itself? What form does it take? Above I cited in passing Jung's statement about our "meeting ourselves … in a thousand disguises on the path of life." Succinctly descriptive of the self-othering, self-encountering character of the soul, this text, I submit, is entirely in keeping with the text I just quoted in which the psychologist is encouraged to wander with a human heart through the world, and previous to that, the one about psychology finding more of itself in the other disciplines. Pulling all this together, the point to be grasped is that whichever way we venture forth, be it into a setting such as Jung describes or into the findings of another field, "we cannot go beyond ourselves [i.e., to some Archimedean point outside—G.M] but only deeper into ourselves," which is also to say, into a form of subjectivity that, as Jung puts it, "is not identical with the ego *because in this self we appear wondrously strange to ourselves.*"[55] It's the very same point that Jung makes in his "Commentary to 'The Secret of the Golden Flower'" when he declares that: "A growing familiarity with the spirit of the East should be taken merely as a sign that we are beginning to relate to the alien elements within ourselves."[56] And then there is the statement he made with respect to the "unexpectedly dark brother" that a European such as himself encounters when travelling in North Africa, India, etc.: "and though I deny it a thousand times, *it is also in me.*"[57]

Expressed in the words of our novelist, this other-mediated self-experience, which Jung describes as strange and alien, corresponds to, or more than that is the same as, what in his little essay on art Conrad apostrophizes with our phrase "that glimpse of truth for which you had forgotten to ask."

Examples are legion. We have only to think of the figures that show up in our dreams, of the people who have made a soulful impression upon us during the course of our lives, of the characters in a play or a novel. Each of these may exemplify, personify, a truth or facet thereof that has not been recognized before. In this connection, consider again the just mentioned "unexpectedly dark brother" that the European meets in his travels. Surely, what Jung had in mind when he wrote of this was the soul-stirring impression that the sight of a majestic horseman had once made upon him during his own travels in North Africa. Shortly after his having seen this proud horseman ride past him at the oasis of Nefta in Tunisia,[58] Jung had a dream in which he finds himself in a life and death struggle with a figure of the same appearance.[59] The action of the dream, which in its first part consists of his fighting with this dark prince in a moat filled with water, Jung aptly compares to the biblical story of Jacob's wrestling with an angel at the river ford.[60] Reflecting upon this North African travel experience and upon the dream it gave rise to, Jung insightfully surmises that he had "unconsciously wanted to find that part of [his] personality which had become invisible under the influence and pressure of being European."[61] Commenting further, he speaks about how the "seemingly alien and wholly different Arab surroundings awaken an archetypal memory of an only too well known prehistoric past which is entirely forgotten."[62] It was this "potentiality of life which has been overgrown by civilization, but which in certain places is still existent,"[63] that he believed himself to have grappled with in the guise of the Arab. Of course, Jung well knew that the life potential mediated by this figure could not be naively relived. Such "playing native," as we call it, would not do.[64] But he also insisted that such experiences, constituting as they do "a clash with the shadow of the self,"[65] were worth bearing in mind and reflecting upon. In the horseman that had passed by so impressively, as in the struggle with the figure of the dark prince in his subsequent dream, his travels in North Africa had been glimpsed from within even as at the same time the psychological consciousness that he as Archimedeanless traveller had so wholeheartedly been the exponent of appeared wonderfully strange to itself.[66]

For my next example of this self-othering, or as it may now also be called, familiar-made-strange, strange-made-familiar form of insight, I turn to Conrad. Writing of the experience that served to inspire his great novel *Lord Jim*, Conrad tells of the impression that was made upon him by a hapless, yet somehow still stalwart-looking young man he had glimpsed in passing: "One morning in the commonplace surroundings of an Eastern roadstead, I saw his form pass by— appealing—significant—under a cloud [= in trouble, disfavour, or disgrace]—perfectly silent. Which is as it should be. It was for me, with all the sympathy of which I was capable, to seek fit words for his meaning. He was 'one of us.'"[67] Such a tiny encounter, merely the sight of a young man walking down the road. And yet, just as the sight of the horseman riding past him during his travels in Tunisia served to inspire the dream of Jung's we mentioned, and just as for Proust the taste of madeleine cake, dunked in tea, served to inspire his novelist's reverie in the case of his great novel, *Remembrance of Things Past*, so for Conrad, the sight of this young man was subsequently quickened in his imagination to become the figure of Jim, the young ship's officer of his *Lord Jim*.

There is no need to précis here this masterpiece of Conrad's beyond saying that it explores the character and subsequent fate of a young sailor who was stripped of his credentials as a seaman after being found guilty of professional misconduct at a mariner's inquest. For our purposes it is enough to cite a few statements that are made about this Jim character's self-othering, truth-mediating significance through the mouthpiece of another character of the novel, the venerable Captain Marlow. Attending at the inquest, Marlow makes a comment in which he compares his fellow audience members, many of whom are colleagues of his in the merchant marine, with the defendant, Jim. Inverting what might ordinarily have been expected from such a comparison, he says of his fellow attendees that they "seemed to me strange, foreign, *as if* belonging to some other order of beings I had no connection with. It was only when my eyes turned towards Jim that I had a sense of not being alone of my kind, as if we two had wandered in from some distant regions, from a different world. I turned to him for fellowship. He alone seemed to look natural."[68] In this passage, which Conrad deleted from his final manuscript (possibly because it made his point too blatantly), Marlow describes how estranged from his fellows he feels owing to what on the other side of the same coin is the uncanny affinity he feels with Jim.[69] This sentiment, I believe, reflects Conrad's awareness of being, if only very subtly, something of an outlier himself. Who but he would have wasted a thought on the likes of Jim, let alone attempted to fathom the universality of Jim as an exemplary man of those values-upending times? But fathom he did. In a key passage of the novel, Conrad gives voice to this main thrust of his authorial intent through

Marlow's reaction to having just heard from Jim a detailed account of the circumstances that had led to his failure as a sailor:

> It seemed to me I was being made to comprehend the Inconceivable—and I know of nothing to compare to the discomfort of such a sensation. I was made to look at the convention that lurks in all truth and on the essential sincerity of falsehood. He appealed to all sides at once—to the side turned perpetually to the light of day, and to the side of us which, like the other hemisphere of the moon exists stealthily in perpetual darkness, with only a fearful ashy light falling at times on the edge. He swayed me. I own to it, I own up. The occasion was obscure, insignificant— what you will: a lost youngster, one in a million—but then he was one of us; an incident as completely devoid of importance as the flooding of an ant-heap, and yet the mystery of his attitude got hold of me as though he had been an individual in the forefront of his kind, as if the obscure truth involved were momentous enough to affect mankind's conception of itself ...[70]

And what is this "obscure truth ... momentous enough to affect mankind's conception of itself ..."? Since I have examined this question in detail on another occasion,[71] I will only say in passing here that it had broadly do to with the change in the definition of man which was consequent upon the Industrial Revolution. Prior to that, when ships were powered by the wind, the sense of duty was backed up by centuries of tradition and was utterly sacrosanct. But with the advent of steam power (and I should also mention the ideas concerning the death of god and the insights of Darwin that were also taking hold at that time) all this changed. Less bound by Duty (with a capital D!), men thenceforth lived more and more on their own account—as alienated individuals. And it is this, I propose, that Conrad provides an early glimpse of in his depiction of Jim: the end of Western man's containment in traditional meaning and the birth of what Jung would latter call "modern man in search of a soul."[72]

My next example, also from Conrad's authorship, again has to do with a statement made about a character who at that time was considered a most unlikely subject matter.[73] A few years before he wrote *Lord Jim*, Conrad published another novel, *The Nigger of the Narcissus*. The black man referred to in the title of this great novel of the sea is the black sailor, James Wait, who is depicted in its pages as work-shirking and sickly. A figure of controversary for all on board, due to it being unclear if he is malingering or truly ill, the black Wait negatively mediates the inwardness of that "unavoidable solidarity … which binds men to each other and all mankind to the visible world," which Conrad in his essay on art (published as the preface of this very novel!) said it is the aim of art to depict. Now I speak of a *negative* mediation of inwardness because, when writing about the James Wait character in the preface to the American addition of his *Works*, Conrad states that "in the book he is nothing; he is merely the centre of the ship's collective psychology and the pivot of the action."[74] This, I insist, is a most important statement. Especially for us as psychologically-minded readers,[75] the notion of a character who is nothing, or the other way around, of a nothing that has the form of a character (Shakespeare, we may recall, wrote of a "nothing that almost sees miracles"[76]), is well worth considering more deeply. But let us back up. The immediate context of this line is Conrad's having just discussed the real-life model of this figure in the preceding paragraph. Back in the time of his own days as a sailor, Conrad had had much to do with a black shipmate. Not surprisingly, this real-life James Wait was very much isolated and alone. As Conrad observes, "A negro in a British forecastle is a lonely being. He has no chums." And yet, this fellow, as isolated as he was, became—though here, I suspect, the recollecting Conrad may be getting ahead of himself to what he later made of this character in his novel—the galvanizing foil for the solidarity of all owing to the pathetic figure he cut as a piteous, dying man. As Conrad somewhat obscurely put it, "afraid of death and making her his accomplice, [Wait] was an imposter of some character—mastering our compassion, scornful of our sentimentalism, triumphing over our suspicions."[77]

So much, then, for what Conrad gives us about the real-life model for his James Wait character. The important thing, as Conrad goes on to point out in the sentence we are considering, is not who outside the novel this figure factually was, but rather his being in its pages nothing in his own right, nothing in himself, but rather and at the same time, both less and more than that (!), the negative precipitate of the entire *mise en scène*, or as Conrad puts it, "the centre of the collective psychology and the pivot of its action." What I am driving at here is pretty much the same as what Hegel meant by sublation. Clarifying this concept in his *Science of Logic*, Hegel explains that whereas "[n]othing is *immediate*; what is sublated … is the result of *mediation*; it is a nonbeing but as a *result* which has its origin in a being. It still has, therefore, *in itself* the *determinateness from which it originates*."[78] It is the same, I contend, with the title character of *The Nigger of the Narcissus*. Although he is nothing in the novel, as Conrad avers, this nothing that he is is "a result which has its origins in a being"—not mind you, in the being of his alleged real life model, but in what Conrad in his essay on art called the "passing phase of life" that in a moment of courage the artist snatches "from the remorseless rush of time."[79]

How else could it be? James Wait did not join the crew from outside the novel. On the contrary, like those hands in the Escher etching that produce themselves by drawing one another, he was mustered up from within it. Said another way, being nothing in the book, and yet the centre of its collective psychology and the pivot of its action, the sickly Wait languishing in his hammock reflects that self-negation of what may be called "the all hands on deck" spirit of that "passing phase of life" that Conrad had lived through in his previous career as a sailor and now looked back upon as an author. Though the *Narcissus* was a commercial sailing ship and not a steamer, such sailing brigs, as I noted earlier, were at that time becoming obsolete and giving way to steam vessels, even as in the novel the cook who nurses the dying Wait talks to him about steamboats and the new generation of sailors (if they can still be called that!) who work down in the stokehold shoveling coal into the furnace like fiends.[80] The picture here is one of hellish demoralization. Already redolent of the vicissitudes of this degrading transition (it is one thing to serve a majestic wind-powered ship, quite another to shovel coal into a boiler[81]), Wait becomes the pathetic touchstone or inverted rallying point of the crew's mutinous revolt against their own demise, which is already seen from within as him. Where before, hoisting sails and scrambling up and down the rigging, there had been soul-dignity in the life of a sailor, now in the coal-shoveling industrial age there was a disgruntled, at times mutinous, clamoring for workers' rights. As the narrator puts it on behalf of the crew, "[Wait] was demoralizing. Through him we were becoming highly humanized, tender, complex, excessively decadent: we understood the subtlety of his fear, sympathised with all his repulsions, shirkings, evasions, delusions—as though we had been overcivilized, and rotten, and without any knowledge of the meaning of life."[82] And yet it is not quite as the narrator suggests, that the crew were becoming all these things because of some external deleterious influence exerted upon them by James Wait. Poetically seen through, it is rather the other way around, a matter of the historical situation of that time showing itself from within as the sickly black sailor James Wait.[83] Wait, it follows, is the doppelgänger of that "uncanniest of all guests," the "Nihilism [that] stands at the door"[84] of the Modern era that Nietzsche had written of a decade earlier. For, indeed, just as in *The Will to Power* Nietzsche had spoken of the coming nihilism, Conrad in *The Nigger of the Narcissus* writes of the mutinous voyage of a crew who, having become "overcivilized, and rotten, and without any knowledge of the meaning of life," were no longer at one with their duties as sailors, but had come to begrudge their work and service. An era was closing, dying like James Wait. And it was in the closing of that great era that the aptly named *Narcissus* sailed.[85]

VII

At the outset of this paper I established the psychological difference as the difference between the tremendous amount that psychology knows about "the facts of life" and what Conrad in his essay on art calls "that glimpse of truth for which you had forgotten to ask." Following upon this, I then envisioned an approach to psychotherapy "that is not limited to what is 'going on under the hood,' …, in the world-less machinations of [the patient's] clinically-isolated inner, but that transcending itself as this takes into its purview what may variously be called his *mise en scène*, life-world, or apperceptive surround." More speculative (in the philosophical sense) than empirical, this uroboric approach, as I like to call it,[86] takes seriously Jung's insight into the Archimedeanlessness of psychology. It is because what appears at first glance to be merely the objects of consciousness are at the same time as they are that the eyes through which consciousness visits its gaze upon itself,[87] that the true subject is *absolved* from the ordinarily prevailing subject-here/object-there difference of consciousness, the true inner from the abstractly drawn distinction between inner and outer, and the (unconsciously earnest, unbeknownst to himself wilderness-venturing) patient from his half-heartedness. Now with these and the other matters we have been discussing in mind, let us turn for our final reflection to another passage from Jung.

In his essay, "Concerning Rebirth," Jung again brings to life, in a most vivid and inspiring manner, what I have called the *mise en scène* character of the true subject. Echoing the statements I cited earlier from him about "the other picture that looms up" and about "our meeting ourselves … in a thousand disguises on the path of life," etc., he states in the first part of this passage that "When a summit of life is reached, when the bud unfolds and from the lesser the greater emerges, then as Nietzsche says, 'One becomes Two,' and the greater figure, which one always was but which remained invisible, appears to the lesser personality with the force of a revelation."[88] The idea that Jung is conveying here is much the same as what Giegerich was getting at, as we heard earlier, with his discussion of how, when constituted by being really entered, the wilderness (or whatever the situation may be that attains in this way wilderness-character) is no longer experienced as merely an infinite expanse surrounding us on all sides, but shows itself from within, in his example, as Artemis. And in this connection, we can think again of the majestic horseman that became a figure in Jung's dream when he was travelling in North Africa, and of the youth in the one case and the black sailor in the other whose meaning Conrad explored in the novels of his that we mentioned. All these figures are examples of what Jung in "Concerning Rebirth" describes as "the one becoming two" when "a summit of life is reached." All of them—even the black sailor, Wait, who I interpreted as being representative of the inception of nihilism—are instances of what Jung calls "the greater figure, which one always was but which remained invisible."

But there is a wrinkle in the text. Immediately following upon his ecstatic description of the revelation of the greater figure, Jung adopts a moralistic tone. In a voice like that of an Old Testament prophet, he warns reader, colleague, and patient alike that "He who is truly and hopelessly little will always drag the revelation of the greater down to the level of his littleness, and will never understand that the day of judgment for his littleness has dawned," whereas "the man who is inwardly great will know that the long expected friend of his soul, the immortal one, has now really come, 'to lead captivity captive,' that is, to seize hold of him by whom this immortal had always been confined and held prisoner, and to make his life flow into the greater life—a moment of deadliest peril!"[89] No doubt, this further sentence makes for a wonderful addition. Risk and consequence, courage and cowardice are handsomely evoked in it. Reading and re-reading, we may be prompted to think of the situations in life that test us and of those oh so frequent dreams in which the figure of the dreamer tightens up against, or desperately tries to escape from, the setting he is in. But this text may itself be regarded as an example of the situation it describes. Opening as it does the psychological difference (while overcompensating at the same time for what it moralistically gives out as the regressive possibility of this), it, too, can be read weakly, as a mere exhortation to the ego to live large, or read strongly in terms of the soulful dialectic it dramatically unfolds. That this is so stems from the fact that as an exhortation, directive, or message preached, Jung's statement not only treats the "two" that the "one" has become as *abstract alternatives*, but in the manner of a demanding father, provides a kick in the pants in the direction of the greater of these. We should realize, however, that such an intervention or attitude on the part of the analyst is just as unpsychological as is the plea from a patient after a dream has been insightfully explored, or a soulful conversation has been held, to be told what then he should do.[90] The rub here, of course, is that there is no way to get from the ego to the soul. Whatever merit encouragement, coaching, and even a kick in the pants may have in other aspects of the psychotherapeutic work, these are powerless to effect that essential transformation, if transformation it is. Better simply to start in the soul.[91] To stick with the image, the dream, the apperceptive surround, and maybe even to congratulate the patient on the "picture that has loomed up," the scene he is in—this on the understanding that even if he is utterly daunted by that situation or scene, attempting his escape, this only points to his having been reached by it deeply, to its already reflecting the *coniunctio* with soul.[92] For, considered in the light of the situation these are in, "he that is truly and hopelessly little" and "he that is inwardly great," are not different ones, but the same. Which is also to say, that even the coward's part is played out in a landscape of courage. And from this it follows that the true subject is not the courageous one more than the cowardly one of these, but, in keeping with that motto about the greater part of the soul being outside the body,[93] corresponds to the situations and scenes that have gone under and across into further determinations of themselves through them—to the brothels and gambling hells, hospitals, prisons, and revivalist gatherings, etc., into which Jung bid the psychologist to venture, even if such venturing never literally leaves the consulting room, but, bursting out of its confines all the same, is only a matter of how in the patient's material a voice in the wilderness is heard to cry out "I."[94]

VIII

Having given in the previous chapter my final reflection, I shall here only add a brief closing remark. In a letter to his publisher Samuel Taylor Coleridge insightfully observed that "The common end of all *narrative* ... is to make those events, which in real or imagined History move in a *straight* Line [,] assume ... a *circular* motion—the snake with its Tail in its Mouth."[95] In this essay, the circular motion that applies narratives to themselves in the tail-eating manner of the Uroboros symbol alluded to by this poet is that of a uroboric psychotherapy in which the soul-as-subject comes home to itself via what I have variously called its *mise en scène,* life-world, and apperceptive surround.[96] Now with respect to this it is important to emphasize that the Uroboros (or whatever else the essence of our world relation may be called or figured as in specific concrete contexts) is nothing else than the dialectic of its own self-negating self-production.[97] By this I mean that such a snake does not first exist, then to bite its tail, but the other way around, is nothing else than the circular motion of its giving birth to itself—i.e., to the thought as which it is—even as it devours itself. It is the same dialectic that Hegel was getting at with his teaching about what he called the philosophical or speculative sentence.[98] Just as we may find when reading a difficult text (or when listening, for that matter, to what someone is saying to us) that by the time we have gotten to the end of a particular statement or paragraph we must go back to the beginning, perhaps several times, to reconsider what its now changed-up (!) topic or sentence subject was in the first place, so also must the Uroboros chew its tail, and the subjects that we are forget and re-member ourselves in accordance with the situations that have been staged for us as a function of our will to know.[99] And the same can be said with respect to psychotherapy, on the one hand, and that line from Conrad that inspired this essay, on the other. Rounding upon themselves in the same negatively-constituting manner as the Uroboros-serpent (which in Jung's words, "devours, fertilizes, begets, slays and brings itself to life again"),[100] what Conrad called "that truth for which you had forgotten to ask," and Jung "the higher psychotherapy,"[101] are not anything that could be known beforehand and applied from without, such as a fact or value, edict, principle, or theory. On the contrary, it is only *a posteriori*, i.e., in the circularity of its negativity as forgotten and the negation of this as remembered, that such a truth—let's call it in our context, *the truth of psychotherapy*—is glimpsed, produced, seen through to in the first place. "Animae extra corpus est," indeed!

Extensive Endnotes in Lieu of a Seminar

[1] Sendivogius, "De Sulphere," *Musaeum Hermeticum* (1678). Cited by C.G. Jung in his 12 July, 1951 letter to Karl Kerényi, *Letters*, vol. 2, p. 19. See also Jung, *CW* 12 §396, 399.

[2] Joseph Conrad, "The Author's Preface," to *The Nigger of the Narcissus*, New York: The Heritage Press, 1965, pp. xv-xix.

[3] Conrad, "The Author's Preface," p. xv.

[4] C. G. Jung, *CW* 16 § 367

[5] In an important statement Giegerich has criticized modern psychology for having "*willfully and with methodological awareness* rid itself of this entire dimension of truth and made a dogma out of the expulsion of truth from theory ...." In all its variety of kinds and schools, psychology has become "the study of ideas, feelings, experiences, and images, expressly apart from the question of whether they are true or not." Wolfgang Giegerich, *The Soul's Logical Life: Towards a Rigorous Notion of Psychology* (Frankfurt am Main: Peter Lang, 1998), p. 229.

[6] Although this woman had a period of breakdown for which she was hospitalized in the United States, she was not known to Jung personally and was never in his care. For pertinent background see Sonu Shamdasani, "A Woman called Frank," *Spring 50: A Journal of Archetype and Culture*, 1990, pp. 26-56.

[7] Jung, *CW* 5 § 329.
[8] Jung, *CW* 12 § 431.

[9] Cited by Giegerich, *The Soul's Logical Life*, 210. The reference is to Jung, *CW* 9, i: 483.

[10] This in not to say that the Oedipus complex is not as ubiquitous as Freud insisted it is. It is rather to hold with Jung that "Freud makes his theory, so admirably suited to the nature of neurotics—much too dependent on the neurotic ideas from which precisely the patients suffer" (*CW* 5 § 655).

[11] "Psychology does not need and, if it is to *be* psychology, cannot be built upon an *external, underlying* foundation," writes Giegerich. And this goes for the term "soul," too. "The soul must not be naively imagined as the acting agent or already-existing producer, the mastermind, *behind* psychic phenomenology. Rather, the soul is autogenic. The soul *makes* itself ... comes into being through its phenomenology, as the [logically negative] *result* of its productions ..." Giegerich, *CEP* IV, p. 4 and p. 5 respectively.

[12] Giegerich The *Soul's Logical Life*, pp. 111-113, 156.

[13] I mean "speculative" here in the sense of speculative philosophy. In this tradition, concepts such as "soul," "truth," and "justice" are continuously measured against themselves in the situation at hand, which is also to say, defined and redefined via a rigorous process of immanent critique.

[14] The acronym PDI refers to "psychology as the discipline of interiority." See Giegerich, *The Soul's Logical Life*, p. 97: "Psychology is the discipline of interiority. But this interiority is not in me, not in you, not in any*body*, also not in the depth of any thing out there. It is in its (psychology's) own Notion of *itself*."

[15] It is important to grasp that conceptions of psychology or definitions of soul that are based upon the privileging of particular psychic or biological phenomena fall below the mark of a truly *psychological* psychology.

[16] Giegerich, *The Soul's Logical Life*, p. 90. See also Giegerich's reference to having "to drop vertically into the *internal* abyss of the mere *word* soul," p. 95.

[17] For Giegerich's introduction of this term into psychology see his "The Present as a Dimension of the Soul: 'Actual Conflict' and Archetypal Psychology," *CEP* vol. 1, pp. 111-112.

[18] Homer, *The Odyssey,* Book IV.

[19] For more on the soul's wholeness see Giegerich, *The Soul's Logical Life*, pp. 72-74, 117-118, 239.

[20] Matthew 18: 13-15, Luke 15: 1-7, John 10: 7-17.
[21] Matthew 25:40.

[22] Wolfgang Giegerich, "Is the Soul 'Deep?'—Entering and Following the Logical Movement of Heraclitus' 'Fragment 45'." Histories-*Spring 64* (Fall/Winter 1998), p. 19. Also in Giegerich, *CEP,* VI, p, 149.

[23] Matthew 10:29-31.

[24] Referenced by Jung in *CW* 14 § 624, *CW* 11 § 707, *CW* 9, i § 555.

[25] Giegerich, *The Soul's Logical Life*, pp. 118, 203-275.
[26] Giegerich, *The Soul's Logical Life*, pp. 206, 214.

[27] Giegerich, *The Soul's Logical Life*, p. 215.

[28] Jung, *CW* 5 § 276

[29] Conrad, "The Author's Preface" in *The Nigger of the Narcissus*, p. xviii. The concept of "solidarity" was much discussed in Conrad's times, coming into use as an English word in the same year as *The Communist Manifesto* (1848). For more on this topic see Ian Watt, *Conrad in the Nineteenth Century*, Berkeley/Los Angeles: University of California Press, 1979, pp. 109-115. With Conrad's reference to "solidarity" in mind, compare Giegerich's definition of the soul as the world of linguistically-mediated "shared meanings" in his *What Is Soul?* New Orleans, Spring Journal Books, 2012, pp. 29-45, 53, 63, 75. As for Conrad's reference to the "mysterious origin" of the solidarity he is intent on showing, we would not go wrong in also seeing this as a reference to language. Language mediates all human activity and is the origin of solidarity. And it is this that the literary artist makes explicit— in itself and for itself.

[30] C. G. Jung, *The Visions Seminars: Book One*, Zürich: Spring Publications, 1976, p. 8.

[31] Jung writes of the "[unconsciously] staged," "*mise en scène*" character of hysterical attacks (*CW* 4 § 364), and Giegerich, likewise, of the *mise en scène* character of neurosis (his *Neurosis: The Logic of a Metaphysical Illness*, New Orleans, Spring Journal Books, 2013, pp. 26, 28, 50, 278, 341, 366, 376, 397, 401). Not restricted to hysteria and neurosis, my use of the term in this paper is more in keeping with Shakespeare's lines from *As You Like It:* "All the world's a stage, and all men and women merely players" (Act II, Scene VII). Of course, this wider, non-neurotic conception can also be found in Jung and Giegerich. When Jung, for example (though in a somewhat different context), writes

that "The whole man is challenged and enters the fray with his total reality" (*MDR*, p. 337), we can readily understand that the whole man referred to is not some big, well-rounded guy, who then secondarily steps into the fray, but, whatever his size or shape, is just as much defined, reflected, and produced by (and indicative, reflective, and productive of!) the entirety of his *mise en scène* or apperceptive surround. With regards to Giegerich, we can think in this connection of his shift away from psychology as the study of what goes on inside people in favor of "the wild" which, as we already heard from him, is constituted by entering one's situation so whole-heartedly that it is seen from within in its essence.

[32] My point here is not that the dream's imagery, *per se*, is the other picture. To get to the other picture we have to see-through the dream to "the soul" by thinking the unity of the unity and difference of the various aspects of the dream.

[33] Jung, *CW* 8 § 316. I like to compare this text of Jung's with Nietzsche's statement: "It is a good ability to be able to observe one's condition with an artistic eye and even in pain and suffering, awkwardness, and matters of that sort to have the Gorgon gaze that instantaneously petrifies everything into a work of art: that gaze from a realm without pain." Cited in Rüdiger Safranski, *Nietzsche: A Philosophical Biography*, Shelly Frisch, trans., New York: W.W. Norton & Company, 2002, p. 27.

[34] W.B. Yeats, "The Sorrow of Love" in *Yeats: Selected Poetry*, London: Macmillan, 1974, p.17.

[35] Jung, *CW* 16 § 173.
[36] Jung, *CW* 16 § 174.
[37] Jung, *CW* 16 § 174.

[38] Blind to the psychological difference, and yet widely advertised by referring physicians who know nothing about it beyond having been trained to recommend it, Cognitive Behaviour Therapy ("CBT") deserves mention here as the exemplar of a soul-less form a treatment focussing narrowly and literalistically upon the psychic sphere of what I here call "the clinically isolated inner."

[39] Compare Giegerich, "The *soul* is always 'outside,' all around us and around everything, because it is the syntax or the logic of life, and 'inside' it is only in the sense and to the extent that as such it also permeates us and everything in our world." His *What Is Soul?* New Orleans, Spring Journal Books, 2012, p. 324. See also Jung: "Everyday life is at bottom an extensive and greatly varied association experiment; in principle we react in one as we do in the other" (*CW* 4 § 700).

[40] Dreams present a *mise en scène,* a staged scene with various figures. The dream-I, it is important to emphasize, is not the psychological I. The psychological I is only produced by and as the interpretation of the dream. The dream-I has to be comprehended as being at one with itself in its others—with the other figures and features of the dream— to be the psychological I.

[41] "Psychological induction," writes Jung, "inevitably causes the two parties to get involved in the transformation of the third and to be themselves transformed in the process" (*CW* 16 § 399).

[42] Giegerich has cautioned that amplifications can be so facile and familiar that their mediation of our seeing-through to the soul cannot be taken at face value, but must be seen-through again, a second time. For his important discussion of this topic see his *Neurosis: The Logic of a Metaphysical Illness*, New Orleans: Spring Journal Book, 2013, pp. 176-177, ft. 118.

[43] Jung writes, "As I see it, the psyche is a world in which the ego is contained" (*CW* 13: 75). "You rightly emphasize that man in my view is enclosed in *the* psyche (not in *his* psyche). 14 May 1950, Letter to Joseph Goldbrunner.

[44] "… we place the patient and his life in the dream," writes Hillman. "Our first psychotherapeutic move is to imagine him in a dream. His dayworld stories are regarded as further places where his dream is dreamt, his problems further analogies to his images." James Hillman, *The Dream and the Underworld*, New York: Harper & Row, 1979), p. 195.

[45] Jung, *CW* 16 § 534. Compare Jung's statement: "…the self comprises infinitely more than a mere ego, as the symbolism has shown from of old. It is as much one's self, and all other selves, as the ego. Individuation does not shut one out from the world, but gathers the world to oneself" (*CW* 8 § 432).

[46] Jung, *CW* 9, i § 112.
[47] Jung, *CW* 16 § 209.

[48] 17 June, 1957, Letter to Benjamin Nelson, C. G. Jung, *Letters*, vol. 2, p. 307.

[49] Cited by Sonu Shamdasani, *Jung and the Making of Modern Psychology: The Dream of a Science*, Cambridge: Cambridge University Press, 2003, p. 22.

[50] Jung, *Letters* 2, p. 307. 17 June 1956, to Nelson.

[51] Jung, *CW* 8 § 752. See also Jung's statement, "Although we are specialists par excellence, our specialized field, oddly enough, drives us to universality and to complete overcoming of the specialist attitude …" (*CW* 16 § 190).

[52] Jung, *CW* 8 § 661 (transl. modified).
[53] Jung, *CW* 7 § 409.

[54] Compare here the Buddhist teacher Trung-pa's saying: "Situations are my guru."

[55] To Ewald Jung, 31 July, 1935, *Letters*, vol. I, p. 193. My italics.

[56] Jung, *CW* 13 § 72.
[57] Jung, *CW* 18 § 1472.
[58] Jung, *MDR*, p. 240.
[59] Jung, *MDR*, pp. 242-246.

[60] Genesis 32:22-32. This passage is not only apt as an amplification highlighting the archetypal status of Jung's dream of wrestling with the Arab. It is also illustrative of what in PDI is called speculative self-relation. When a particular subject or subject matter meets itself in another figure, the upshot of this may be its redefinition and renaming. In the biblical story, Jacob does not cease from struggling with the angel, even after his hip is wrenched from its socket. "I will not let you go unless you bless me," he declares. In response to this the angel then blesses him with a new name. "Your name will no longer be Jacob, but Israel, because you have struggled with God and with humans and have overcome." Notice that the name is changed from a mere given name to a universal name, the name of an entire people. In Jung's story the subtle parallel to this is Jung's having cast himself in the role of European Man. It is not merely as the person, Carl Jung, but as European Man, that he encounters the Arab culture of North Africa.

[61] Jung, *MDR*, p. 244.
[62] Jung, *MDR*, pp. 245-246.
[63] Jung, MDR, p. 246.

[64] It is worth recalling that Jung was a strong critic of what we now call cultural appropriation. He decries in the strongest terms the idea that one can "put on, like a new suit of clothes, ready-made symbols grown on foreign soil, saturated in foreign blood, spoken in a foreign tongue, nourished by a foreign culture, interwoven with foreign history," for to do so would be to "resemble a beggar who wraps himself in a kingly raiment …" (*CW* 9, i § 27) And yet when grappling with figures such as that of the Arab prince of his dream, he did "aim …, through insight, to make [what was in this way mediated] more conscious, so that … a common modus vivendi" could be found (*MDR*, p. 244.). The superseding subtly of mind that for Jung reconciles these seemingly opposed positions resides in his emphasis upon *our appearing strange to ourselves* in the figure of or foil of the other. When read in the light of one another, two statements of Giegerich's are helpful in this connection. Firstly: "But for psychology there is no Other. Or the other that there is is 'the soul's own other, its internal other, itself *as* other. 'The soul' is self-relation" (Giegerich, et. al., *Dialectics and Analytical Psychology: The El Capitan Canyon Seminar*, New Orleans: Spring Journal Books, 2005, p. 26). Secondly: "The psychological question is not, cannot be, what and how the soul *is*, but how the soul is reflected in its manifestations. … psychology is the study of the *reflection* in some mirror and not the study of *what* the mirror is the reflection *of*" (*CEP* vol. VI, p. 132). But having cited these texts I should immediately add that with the move from Jung's account of his North African experience to Giegerich and PDI we are also moving from an emphasis on personality development (Jung thinks of the figure of the other as mediating parts of his personality that had been blotted out by an adapted persona) to an emphasis on the development of consciousness via the cognition of truth.

[65] Jung, *MDR*, p. 246.

[66] The only problem with this story of Jung's for what I am attempting to show here is his having construed its significance in terms of personality development, rather than in terms of truth. It might be argued, of course, that the truth involved had to do with the insight Jung drew from this experience with respect to his hypothesis of the collective unconscious. And in this connection, I am reminded of a line from Conrad's novel, *The Heart of Darkness* (Hammondsworth: Penguin Books, 1983). Just as Jung's sighting of that Arab horseman during his North African travels was edifying with respect to this signature idea of his, so the protagonist of this novel sees in the "wild and passionate uproar" of tribal dancing in the African jungle what he calls "truth stripped of its cloak of time" (p. 69). But here we should realize that the collective unconscious has only the status of an empirical hypothesis about the alleged present currency of former truths in the psyche of individuals and is not itself a truth. Not even if empirically verified, would it have truth character. Truths—soul truths—are existing concepts, the logic at the heart of our world relation, of life as it is actually lived. Appearing principally in the way things are named, they are the universals that may be seen, seen through to, and exemplified in particular phenomena. Expressed in another formulation, soul truths are insights speculatively produced by, or rather as, the reverberatingly uroboric bodying-forth of Archimedeanlessness. As for Conrad's line about "truth stripped of its cloak of time," while this nicely indicates the commonality of human nature everywhere, the *truths* of human cultural life, of soul life, are always a function of time, and can hardly be stripped of it. Which is why, after Conrad gives a very rich description of the strange kinship that the protagonist of this novel feels with the wild African dancers, he has him explain that, despite the allure of doing so, he did not join the dancers because, as he puts it, "I had no time. I had to … put bandages on those leaky steam-pipes" (pp. 69-70). It is highly noteworthy that the new truth—the age of steam—becomes leaky and

44

in need of repair when the African dancers are seen! I take this to mean that against resistances the new truth has to be explicitly allowed to be true. As the protagonist declares, "Let the fool [at the dancers] gape and shudder—the man knows, and can look on without a wink. ... he [knows he] must at least be as much of a man as these on shore [i.e., as much the whole man as they!]. He must meet that truth with his own true stuff—with his own inborn strength" (p. 69). In contrast to Jung's account of his wrestling with the figure of the Arab in his dream, Conrad's protagonist in this passage struggles, not so much to integrate the chthonic shadow (though some credence may be given to this interpretation), as to overcome his resistance to the new truth of the Industrial Age.

[67] Joseph Conrad, *Lord Jim*, Cedric Watts & Robert Hampson, eds., London: Penguin Books, 1986, p. 44.

[68] Cited in Ian Watt, *Conrad in the Nineteenth Century*, Berkeley/Los Angeles: University of California Press, 1979, p. 316.

[69] A passage from Hegel is worth citing in connection to Marlow's identification with Jim and their subsequently becoming friends: "…it is the character of the person, the subject, to surrender its isolation and separateness. Ethical life, love, means precisely the giving up of particularity, of particular personality, and its extension to universality—so, too, with 'friendship.' In friendship and love I give up my abstract personality and thereby win it back as concrete. The truth of personality is found precisely in winning it back through this immersion, this being immersed in the other." G. W. F. Hegel, *Lectures on the Philosophy of Religion*, One-Volume Edition, The Lectures of 1827, Peter C. Hodgson, ed., R.F. Brown, P.C. Hodgson, and J.M. Stewart, trans., Berkeley: University of California Press, 1988, pp. 427-428.

[70] Conrad, *Lord Jim*, pp. 111-112.

[71] Greg Mogenson, *Dereliction of Duty and the Rise of Psychology: As Reflected in the "Case" of Conrad's Lord Jim*. Published by The International Society for Psychology as the Discipline of Interiority, Monograph Series, volume one.

[72] That the disgraced sailor, Jim, is able to be taken up as the subject matter of a great novel is already a sign of a new man.

[73] Early critics of Conrad's *The Nigger of the Narcissus* objected that the book belonged to "the school of fiction-brutality," one reviewer saying of its characters that they were "generally worthless characters." Cited in Ian Watt, *Conrad in the Nineteenth Century*, Berkley and Los Angeles: University of California Press, 1979, p. 127.

[74] Cited from Conrad's 1914 preface to the American edition of his *Works* by Howard Mumford Jones in his "Introduction" to Conrad's *The Nigger of the Narcissus*, p. viii.

[75] By "psychologically-minded readers" I mean readers who look to literature as the speculative predicate or internal other of psychology, that is, as psychology redoubled, psychology a second time. For a discussion of this see my *Dereliction of Duty and the Rise of Psychology*.

[76] William Shakespeare, *King Lear* II. 2. 165.

[77] Cited from Conrad's 1914 preface to the American edition of his *Works* by Howard Mumford Jones in his "Introduction" to Conrad's *The Nigger of the Narcissus*, p. viii. I take Conrad's characterization of his black shipmate as having made death his accomplice as meaning that he succumbed to his fear of death. Compare here the fuss that the

James Wait character in the novel makes about dying and the reaction of the venerable old sailor, Singleton, to this: "'Well, get on with your dying,' he said with venerable mildness; 'don't raise a blamed fuss with us over that job'" (p. 42). With regards to the idea of Wait being an "imposter of some character," I read this to mean that, like his character in the novel, he was regarded by Conrad as a negative exemplar of the universal.

[78] G.W. F. Hegel, *Hegel's Science of Logic*, A.V. Miller, trans., New York: Humanity Books, 1999, p. 107.

[79] Conrad, "The Author's Preface" in *The Nigger of the Narcissus*, p. xviii.
[80] Conrad, *The Nigger of the Narcissus*, p. 107.

[81] In another novel written late in his career, Conrad recalls how as a young sailor he once impetuously quit a job: "For no reason on which a sensible person could put a finger I threw up my job—chucked my berth—left the ship of which the worst that could be said was that she was a steamship and therefore, perhaps, not entitled to that blind loyalty which …"—the reader is meant to complete the sentence by thinking of majestic sailing ships and the loyalty they inspire. See Joseph Conrad, *The Shadow-Line*, New York: Vintage Books, 2007, p. 4.
[82] Conrad, *The Nigger of the Narcissus*, p. 130. Conrad's reference to the sailors being "without any knowledge of the meaning of life" is a euphemistic phrase for the decline of their sense of duty. Rooted in Tradition, duty is the meaning of a sailor's life.

[83] An implication of these insights for work in the consulting room. Although Jung insisted "that one dreams in the first place, and almost to the exclusion of all else, of oneself" (*CW* 10: 321), it is important to remain open to the possibility that the figure of the other can be read,

not merely for what it contributes to the personality, but for what it figuratively indicates with respect to the logic of one's world relation (usually at an *opus parvum* level, maybe for some at a greater level sometimes). Rather than claiming to have met *oneself* in the other, the thrust of this interpretative alternative would be to attempt to fathom how it might be said of a particular figure, who is uncanny with surplus value, that (as Conrad said of the title character of his *The Nigger of the Narcissus* novel), "in the book [or one's life] he is nothing; he is merely the centre of the ship's collective psychology and the pivot of the action," i.e., the face of a shared meaning. It seems to me that in listening to our patients' narratives and dreams, we can leave the personality behind for the landlubbers, and launch out into the sea of this interpretative possibility. The person discussed, the third party or the dream figure, is then nothing but a negative precipitate of one's world relation's having been implicitly thought, or again, the figuring or personification of the concept or logic that one exists as, i.e., the perhaps homely, or apple of discord bearing, *spiritus rector* (sometimes tightened up against, rejected, or scapegoated, sometimes menacingly imposing) that encompasses and suffuses the mind and the real as one. Not a part of me, of my personality, but the Archimedeanless view from within bodied forth as this figure. Now, about such "personified intellectual intuitions," as these might be called, something more can be learned from another great novelist. In his novel, *The Unbearable Lightness of Being*, Milan Kundera has his narrator state that "It would be senseless for the author to try to convince the reader that his characters once really lived. They were not born of a mother's womb; they were born of a stimulating phrase or two or from a basic situation" (p. 19). And so it is with the main character of this novel. As the narrator explains, although he had been thinking of Tomas for many years, it was only in the light of his reflecting upon Nietzsche's notion of Eternal Recurrence and his own counter-notion of the unbearable lightness of being that he came to see this character clearly

(p. 6). Milan Kundera, *The Unbearable Lightness of Being*, translated from the Czech by Michael Henry Heim, New York: Harper & Row Publishers, 1984.

[84] Friedrich Nietzsche, *The Will to Power*, Walter Kaufmann & R. J. Hollingdale, trans., New York: Vintage Books, 1968, p. 7.

[85] Psychological insight has less to do with redeeming or re-enchanting something that was once a soul truth, than with letting a position that is no longer the truth of a person's or a people's present reality be explicitly set aside and departed from. In keeping with this, Giegerich (*CEP* vol. V, p. 31) has quoted a statement from Roland Barthes: "To be modern means to know what is no longer possible." We can also think here of Hegel's famous line from the Preface of his *Philosophy of Right*: "When philosophy paints its grey in grey [i.e., comprehends matters theoretically], then has a shape of life grown old. By philosophy's grey in grey it cannot be rejuvenated but only understood. The owl of Minerva spreads its wings only with the falling of the dusk." In clinical work all this corresponds to the working through of resistances. As Jung puts it, "The chief obstacle to new modes of psychological adaptation is conservative adherence to the earlier attitude" (*CW* 4 § 350).

[86] The adjective "uroboric" descriptively draws upon the symbol of the uroboros, the serpent with its tail in its mouth. It is a very apt representation of what can variously be called Archimedeanless self-relation, speculative thinking, dialectics, the *form* of self, as well as for that mode of interpretation that aims to interiorize phenomena into themselves (rather than viewing them from an external perspective) and that grasps the universal in the particular. Giegerich writes: "Psychotherapy that deserves the predicate 'theoretical' is committed to the Serpent. Even while sitting in the 'clinical' atmosphere of the

consulting room and concentrating on this real, empirical patient, it is nevertheless reached by, and itself touches, what the patient and the consulting room are *not*: their 'more,' their logical negativity, the world-encircling Serpent" (*The Soul's Logical Life*, p. 68). For a related discussion of the felicity of the uroboros symbol for psychology as the discipline of interiority see Giegerich, *CEP* III, pp. 3-4.

[87] Jung (*MDR*, p. 50) writes of a kind of "'insight' ... based on instinct, or on a *'participation mystique'* with others. It is as if the 'eyes of the background' do the seeing in an impersonal act of perception." See as well his citation from the alchemist, Dorneus, "There is in natural things a certain truth not seen by the outward eye but perceived by the mind alone. Of this the philosophers had experience ..." (*CW* 11 § 152, note 47).

[88] Jung, *CW* 9, i § 217.
[89] Jung, *CW* 9, i § 217.

[90] The request to be told what to do is a resistance. Instead of simply acknowledging or being convicted by the truth that has been glimpsed, the patient drives a wedge between himself and his truth by asking what he should now do. At such a juncture, what can be said, short of obliging his request, is that, having dreamt this dream or having had this insight, it is most likely that his subsequent decisions and choices, whatever these may be, will proceed apace upon the basis of who he has already now thereby become. Cf. *CW* 12 § 37 for Jung's comments on patients' asking what they should do.

[91] On this topic Giegerich has importantly pointed out that "A *real* psychology of the Self has to *start out* from the *accomplished* Self, otherwise there can be no Self-development." Elaborating, he continues, "You have to already be there if you want to get there. You

have to have arrived before you set out on the way that is to take you to where you want to arrive. On this *hysteron proteron* hinges the whole question of realness (actuality) or irreality of psychological work" (*The Soul's Logical Life*, p. 21). See also Giegerich, *What Is Soul?*, p. 304.

[92] A point made by Giegerich in "The Dream in Psychotherapy, Its Role and Significance," unpublished paper.

[93] The alchemical motto appearing as an epigraph at the top of this essay, *"maior autem animae extra corpus est."* For Giegerich's important comment about this statement as "a statement that, if accepted, makes a personalistic conception of psychology impossible," see his *The Soul's Logical Life*, p. 40, note. 24.

[94] Logically negative, the "I" referred to here is the *result* of the absolute exposure of consciousness or the subject to its *mise-en-scène* or apperceptive surround. Or, putting this differently, it (*sic!*) is the logically negative *result* of what Jung has called the "unconscious collusion" of the patient's whole environment with him (*CW* 16 § 194). Pertinent in this connection is Jung's statement, "The meaning of my existence is that life has addressed a question to me. Or, conversely, I myself am a question which is addressed to the world, and I must communicate my answer. That is the suprapersonal life task, which I accomplish only by effort and with difficulty" (*MDR*, p. 318). Commenting on these lines, Giegerich adds, "Life as such *is* the question. It has in itself question quality. … I have to, my life has to, *be* the answer to the question that I am called upon to answer" (*The Soul's Logical Life,* p. 75). We can also think here of a statement made by Marx. Drawing upon Hegel's alteration of the motto *Hic Rhodus, hic saltus* [= here is Rhodes, here jump] to be read as "Here is the Rose, dance thou here," Marx writes, "a situation is created which makes all turning back impossible, and the conditions themselves call out: *Hic*

Rhodus, hic salta!" Cited from, Karl Marx, *The Eighteen Brumaire of Louis Bonaparte.*

[95] Letter to Joseph Cottle, 1815. Cited in Mark C. Taylor, *Journeys to Selfhood: Hegel and Kierkegaard,* Berkley: University of California Press, 1980, p. 227.

[96] With respect to the soul-as-subject coming home to itself via its *mise en scène,* life-world, and apperceptive surround, I am reminded of Nietzsche's statement (in chapter 1, section 2 of his *Ecce Homo*) that "… [he who is well turned out] is always in his own company, whether he associates with books, human beings, or landscapes …," this because (as is explained a few lines earlier) "… he collects from everything he sees, hears, lives through, *his* sum: he is a principle of selection, he discards much."

[97] In the first chapter of this essay I deplored the idea prevalent in so much of psychotherapy today "that 'a piece of work' can be done on this issue or that, without the peas ever needing to touch the carrots, or the chickens ever having to come home to roost." Taking the last of these sayings a step further (applying it to itself), it can now be understood that these proverbial chickens did not first exist and then come home to roost (as so many compensatory experiences coming home to an already existing patient or subject). The subject—or more precisely, the true subject—is rather the result to begin with (!) of the *mise en scène's* subject-constituting coming home to itself. As Jung taught us to ask, "Who am I that all this should happen to me?" (*CW* 12 §152).

[98] G. W. F. Hegel, *Phenomenology of Spirit,* A.V. Miller, trans., Oxford: Oxford University Press, 1977, § 63, p. 39. Hegel's account of the speculative sentence may usefully be read in connection with his famous statement about "tarrying with the negative." Just as "the life of the spirit," as Hegel puts it in this passage, "wins its truth only when,

in utter dismemberment, it finds itself" (ibid., § 32, p. 19), so, too, must the reader of philosophical sentences suffer the "dismemberment" of his initial understanding of what he is reading if he is to find into its truth. And here, bringing this to life, we can think as well of the dismembering dialectic that Actaion was subject to when, having ventured into the wild, his having beheld the naked truth as the figure of Artemis bathing is reflected in his being simultaneously torn apart by his own dogs. With respect to this scene, Giegerich writes: "What seems to be done to me by the dogs out there is the workings of my own truth upon me (the dogs are *my* dogs!) Taking place in the 'inverted world' of the soul, the dismemberment is neither extraverted nor introverted experience, but 'intensive': an inner refining, a sublimation, a change of the logical status oneself and one's world are in" (*The Soul's Logical Life,* p. 256). We can also reflect the dialectic of dismemberment to which the reader of speculative sentences is subject in the biblical story of Jacob's wresting with the angel, discussed in endnote 60 above. There the moment of negating dismemberment is represented in the detail of Jacob's hip being dislocated, the logical status change or new truth by his name change. For a fuller account of the pertinence of the speculative sentence for psychotherapy see my book, *Psychology's Dream of the Courtroom,* New Orleans: Spring Journal Books, 2016, pp. 84-105, 109-111.

[99] The uroboric apperception here described is not only "staged" for us as a function of our will to know. More deeply fathomed it is also a function of our existing as consciousness.

[100] Jung, *CW* 12 § 460.
[101] Jung, *CW* 16 § 367.

54

ABOUT THE AUTHOR

Greg Mogenson is a registered psychotherapist and Jungian psycho-analyst practicing in London, Ontario, Canada. He is the editor of The Studies in Archetypal Psychology Series of Spring Journal Books as well as a founding member and Vice-President of The International Society for Psychology as the Discipline of Interiority. The author of numerous articles in the field of analytical psychology, his books include *Dereliction of Duty and the Rise of Psychology: As Reflected in the "Case" of Conrad's Lord Jim*; *Psychology's Dream of the Courtroom*; *A Most Accursed Religion: When a Trauma becomes God*; *Greeting the Angels: An Imaginal View of the Mourning Process*; *The Dove in the Consulting Room: Hysteria and the Anima in Bollas and Jung*; *Northern Gnosis: Thor, Baldr, and the Volsungs in the Thought of Freud and Jung*, and (with W. Giegerich and D. L. Miller) *Dialectics & Analytical Psychology: The El Capitan Canyon Seminar*.

For further information, visit the website at: www.gregmogenson.com

www.ingramcontent.com/pod-product-compliance
Lightning Source LLC
Chambersburg PA
CBHW051236250726

48655CB00006B/2798